HEADLINE SERIES

No. 310   FOREIGN POLICY ASSOCIATION   Spring

Hong Kong and China:
'One Country, Two Systems'?

by Frank Ching

1 Prelude 3

2 The Tiananmen Massacre
   and Its Aftermath 17

3 Transition Years: 1991–96 26

4 Hong Kong's Economy 42

5 Uncertain Future 47

   Talking It Over 60
   Reading List 61

Cover Design: Ed Bohon $5.95

#356/8220

The Author

FRANK CHING, author and journalist, has covered and commented on developments in China and Hong Kong for more than two decades.

A senior editor of the *Far Eastern Economic Review*, Mr. Ching opened *The Wall Street Journal's* bureau in Beijing when the United States and China established diplomatic relations in 1979, and he remained there for four years.

He previously had been on the staff of *The New York Times*, where he was the China area specialist on the foreign news desk in New York. From 1987 to 1992, he wrote a weekly column on developments in Hong Kong, China and Taiwan that appeared in the *South China Morning Post* in Hong Kong, as well as newspapers in Taiwan and Japan.

The Foreign Policy Association

The Foreign Policy Association is a private, nonprofit, nonpartisan educational organization. Its purpose is to stimulate wider interest and more effective participation in, and greater understanding of, world affairs among American citizens. Among its activities is the continuous publication, dating from 1935, of the HEADLINE SERIES. The author is responsible for factual accuracy and for the views expressed. FPA itself takes no position on issues of U.S. foreign policy.

HEADLINE SERIES (ISSN 0017-8780) is published four times a year, Spring, Summer, Fall and Winter, by the Foreign Policy Association, Inc., 470 Park Avenue So., New York, N.Y. 10016. Chairman, Paul B. Ford; President, Noel V. Lateef; Editor in Chief, Nancy Hoepli-Phalon; Senior Editors, Ann R. Monjo and K.M. Rohan; Associate Editor, June Lee. Subscription rates, $20.00 for 4 issues; $35.00 for 8 issues; $50.00 for 12 issues. Single copy price $5.95; double issue $11.25. Discount 25% on 10 to 99 copies; 30% on 100 to 499; 35% on 500 and over. Payment must accompany all orders. Postage and handling: $2.50 for first copy; $.50 each additional copy. Second-class postage paid at New York, N.Y., and additional mailing offices. POSTMASTER: Send address changes to HEADLINE SERIES, Foreign Policy Association, 470 Park Avenue So., New York, N.Y. 10016. Copyright 1996 by Foreign Policy Association, Inc. Design by K.M. Rohan. Printed at Science Press, Ephrata, Pennsylvania. Spring 1995. Published June 1996.

Library of Congress Catalog Card No. 96-85425
ISBN 0-87124-170-6

1

Prelude

HONG KONG came into being in the mid-19th century because Britain wanted an outpost, subject to its own laws and regulations, from which to do business with China. The Opium War (1839–42) provided the opportunity. China at the time tried to enforce a prohibition on the importation of opium, which was sapping the spirits of its people and draining the national treasury of silver. However, the British, the largest opium traders at the time, opposed the ban in the name of free trade. In the resulting war, the Chinese were badly defeated. One of Britain's demands was the cession of the island of Hong Kong, at the time home to a few fishermen. Britain formally acquired Hong Kong in 1842, though it had taken possession the year before.

Hong Kong's main asset was its deep-water harbor, and the

The Foreign Policy Association gratefully acknowledges The Freeman Foundation's support for this issue of the HEADLINE SERIES.

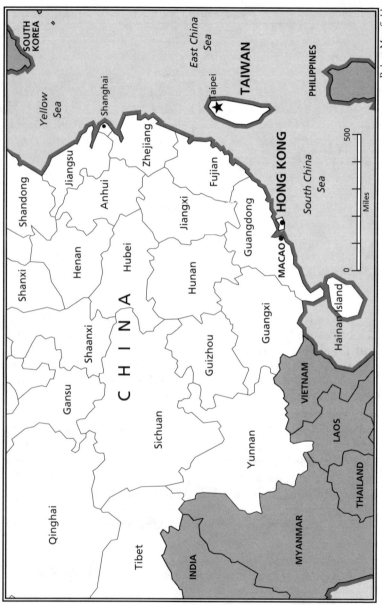

Robert Mansfield

British took advantage of another military encounter in 1860 to make China cede a strip of land on the China mainland that gave them control over both sides of the harbor. Then, in 1898, Britain acquired the rest of what became the colony of Hong Kong, an area known as the New Territories, which accounted for more than 90 percent of the young colony's land area. This third treaty covering the New Territories provided not for ces-

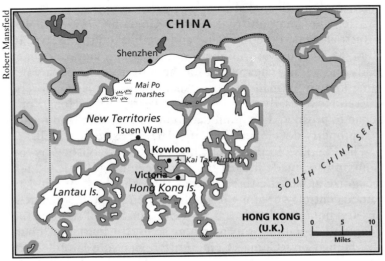

Hong Kong

sion of the land but for a 99-year lease, which in the 19th century must have seemed like perpetuity.

Hong Kong began to attract business people from Britain and other parts of Europe, the United States and China itself. Shipping was its lifeblood, and the harbor constantly received vessels from around the world. It soon became a thriving city. Much of its business involved acting as a middleman in the China trade, facilitating business between the West and China.

Hong Kong also acted as a safety valve for people in China. Whenever the China mainland was convulsed by political upheavals, a stream of refugees would find its way to Hong Kong, beginning with the Taiping Rebellion in the 1850s and continuing through the Japanese invasion of China in the 1930s and the Communist triumph in the civil war of the 1940s. Further waves of refugees flooded into Hong Kong as a result of either political turmoil or starvation on the mainland. The Hong Kong population, by and large, consisted of sojourners from China who were awaiting the chance to return to their homes in Guangdong, Shanghai and other parts.

After the Communist takeover of China in 1949, Shanghai industrialists fled the mainland and established themselves in Hong Kong. The vast numbers of refugees provided a pool of ready and willing cheap labor for them to tap. The colony became known for manufacturing such things as plastic flowers, wigs and textiles. By the late 1960s and early 1970s, Hong Kong began to prosper. The limited amount of available land meant that property developers, in particular, did extremely well.

The People's Republic of China (PRC), established by the Communists, made it clear from the beginning that it did not recognize any of the three treaties through which Britain had gained control over Hong Kong. It dubbed them unequal treaties and hence null and void. However, instead of sending the People's Liberation Army marching across the border to "liberate" Hong Kong, China's Communist rulers were careful not to do anything to change the status quo. Their position was that Hong Kong was a problem left over by history, one that would be solved when the time was ripe.

The Sino-British Negotiations

In the 1950s and 1960s, the British considered 1997 too far removed to be cause for concern. They believed that China recognized the value of Hong Kong's continuing its political and economic system. During the tumult of the Cultural Revolution (1966–76), the British realized that there was no possibility of achieving a reasonable settlement with the radical leadership in Beijing. But the death of Chairman Mao Zedong in 1976, the ending of the Cultural Revolution and the emergence of the pragmatist Deng Xiaoping as China's new supreme leader were thought to provide a window of opportunity. Since Deng was already in his 70s, the British wanted to strike a deal with China while he was still in power.

Moreover, by 1982, with the lease on the New Territories due to expire in 15 years' time, there were practical issues to consider. For one thing, banks had to decide whether they could offer mortgages that extended beyond 1997.

The Chinese at first did not want to address the Hong Kong issue. They had just emerged from 10 years of chaos and had more than enough problems to tackle. But on reflection they decided that they could not formally agree to extend British rule in Hong Kong. It was one thing to turn a blind eye to a situation that had existed for a century and a half. It was quite another for China to sign a new treaty with Britain legitimizing its rule over a part of China.

Historically, Beijing's major concern regarding national reunification had not been Hong Kong but Taiwan. In fact, since Hong Kong provided an opportunity for unofficial contacts with the Chinese Nationalist government which had retreated from the mainland to Taiwan, Beijing's policy had been to keep Hong Kong as it was until the Taiwan issue was resolved. In the early 1980s, Beijing came up with the concept of "one country, two systems," whereby the mainland would continue to practice socialism and Taiwan could retain its capitalist economy. An article was inserted in the Chinese constitution to provide for the setting up of Special Administrative Regions (SARs) that would practice capitalism.

Pressed by Britain to make a decision on Hong Kong, China reversed its priorities. It would reunite with Hong Kong first and apply the concept of "one country, two systems" to that territory. If Taiwan saw that such a policy was successful in Hong Kong, the reasoning went, it would see the benefits of also becoming an SAR.

The Chinese agreed to leave Hong Kong basically unchanged for two reasons—one economic, the other political. Since 1949 Hong Kong had been China's main window on the

THE DIE IS CAST

Hong Kong won't be quite the same after the 1997 handover.

What Will Change

- **Business:** Mainland companies will increase their share of the local economy
- **Military:** Chinese gunboats will be docked in the harbour and PLA troops stationed in the business district
- **Media:** Local and foreign journals will be monitored closely
- **Politics:** The current elected legislature will be dismantled and replaced by a provisional legislature
- **Language:** Chinese will become more and more common in the courts and civil service

What Won't Change

- **Financial status:** Hong Kong will still play a pivotal role as a global financial centre
- **Monetary policy:** Beijing says it won't de-link the Hong Kong currency from the U.S. dollar
- **Borders:** The Hong Kong-China crossing at Shenzhen will remain tightly controlled
- **Entry:** The number of Chinese allowed to enter Hong Kong will continue to be restricted
- **Second-class status:** Major decisions relating to foreign affairs and defence will be taken over Hong Kong's head—but in Beijing rather than London

What's Up for Grabs

- **Law:** Courts could lose their independence
- **Order:** Crime and corruption could skyrocket
- **Taxes:** Rates could shoot up
- **Favouritism:** Government contracts could veer towards mainland firms
- **Freedoms:** Consular protection could be denied to Hong Kong Chinese holding foreign passports
- **Politics:** The pace of democratization towards a fully elected legislature and elected chief executive is undecided
- **Education:** School curriculum could be changed; textbooks are already being revised

Source: Review Data

Far Eastern Economic Review Graphic/Ringo Chung

outside world. With the opening up of China from 1978 on, it was able to do business directly. Still, Hong Kong was the source of much of the mainland's foreign-exchange earnings and the bulk of overseas investments.

Hong Kong was at the time a basically nonpolitical entity. The governor was appointed by the British, and he in turn appointed all the members of the Executive Council and the Legislative Council. The civil service was efficient and did not involve itself in politics. In fact, there was very little politics, since there were no political parties and no elections of any importance. Only the Urban Council, which was responsible for such matters as libraries and garbage collection, had some elected members who sat alongside government appointees. There were also a few pressure groups, one of the most important of which was the Hong Kong Observers, a body formed in 1975 that called not for democracy but for a more accountable government that would give the people of Hong Kong a greater voice in the conduct of public affairs. Its members were mostly well-educated people in their 20s and 30s who had been born in Hong Kong.

The British had not encouraged a democratic system in Hong Kong as it was easier to administer the colony without having to cope with elective politics. In addition, Hong Kong until recent decades had been a society of sojourners, primarily refugees from China who regarded Hong Kong as a way station rather than a permanent home. The political infighting that did exist in Hong Kong was in reality an extension of political divisions within China. After China's civil war, the defeated Nationalists and the Communists continued their verbal warfare, with Hong Kong one of the major arenas for this conflict. There were good reasons for believing in the 1950s and 1960s, and even in the 1970s, that opening up Hong Kong to electoral politics would be an invitation to mainland-based Communists and Taiwan-based Nationalists to slug it out in Hong Kong.

The situation gradually began to change in the 1970s, when a generation of young people born in Hong Kong was coming of age. Prior to then, every census taken by the government had shown that most people in Hong Kong had been born elsewhere. By the late 1980s and 1990s, this new Hong Kong–born generation, with a sense of Hong Kong identity, accounted for the majority of university-educated professionals and managers in the territory. Even without the 1997 issue, there would have been a demand not only for accountability but for democracy.

The Joint Declaration and Its Aftermath

This was not yet obvious in 1984 when the Chinese and the British decided the fate of Hong Kong. China realized the value of Hong Kong and wanted to keep it as an economic entity, with a minimum of political activity. The British explored the possibility of recognizing Chinese sovereignty over Hong Kong in return for being given the right to continue to administer the territory, but the Chinese were not interested. They had decided to take back Hong Kong in 1997, and there was little the British could do to change their minds. Ultimately, the British concentrated their attentions on fleshing out China's policies toward Hong Kong. As a result, the agreement that was unveiled in September 1984, known as the Sino-British Joint Declaration on the Question of Hong Kong, was a much more detailed document than anyone had anticipated.

Under the Joint Declaration, Hong Kong would be allowed to enjoy a high degree of autonomy, and its government would be composed of local inhabitants, with a legislature constituted by elections. (In 1984 all the legislature's members were appointees.) Beijing would not send officials to run Hong Kong; it would not change the former colony's social and economic system and life-style; and it would guarantee existing rights and freedoms. Hong Kong was to remain a free port and an international financial center, and the markets for foreign exchange, gold, securities and futures would continue to function as in the past. There would be no foreign-exchange controls. The Hong Kong dollar would continue to circulate and be freely convertible. Moreover, Hong Kong would have independent finances and would not pay taxes to the central government in Beijing. It could also continue to be a member of international organizations and issue its own travel documents. However, foreign affairs and defense would be handled by Beijing. All these policies, the Joint Declaration said, would remain unchanged for 50 years. China's National People's Congress would encode all these policies in legal form and promulgate a document known as the Basic Law.

The release of this detailed agreement did much to assure people in Hong Kong that the advent of 1997 did not necessarily mean direct Communist control. But there were many skeptics, especially among those who had fled Communist rule on the mainland to find refuge in Hong Kong. They decided that, once again, they had to look for a safe haven, this time outside Hong Kong.

To gauge the Joint Declaration's acceptability to Hong Kong's people, the British set up an Assessment Office. However, they refused to hold a referendum, and no public opinion surveys were commissioned. Members of the public were simply asked to express their views in writing to the Assessment Office. In November, at the end of the consultation period, the Assessment Office prepared a report that said:

> *The provision for the legislature of the Hong Kong SAR [Special Administrative Region] to be constituted by elections was hailed by many…as 'farsighted and progressive.' There should be (as the Hong Kong government plans) a progressive development of a more representative system with seats filled by direct election….The new political structure should be established by the late 80s or early 90s so as to enable Hong Kong people to practice self-administration before 1997…. After the most careful analysis and consideration of all the information received, the office has concluded that most of the people of Hong Kong find the draft agreement acceptable.*

After approval by the British Parliament, the Joint Declaration was formally signed in Beijing by Prime Minister Margaret Thatcher and her Chinese counterpart, Premier Zhao Ziyang, in December 1984.

The Early Transition Period

The first months of the transition exposed the differences in interpretation between the British and Chinese, especially over the thorny issue of representative government. The British took the position that since the legislature was to be fully elected by 1997, gradual steps had to be taken in the intervening 13 years to make the Legislative Council more representative. They began in 1985 by introducing indirect elections to the legislature, as well as functional constituency elections, in which organizations of doctors, lawyers, teachers and others would each choose a representative to the legislature. Their plan was to introduce direct elections in 1988.

Before they could do this, however, China intervened. Xu Jiatun, China's representative in Hong Kong, held an unprecedented news conference during which he accused Britain of violating the Joint Declaration with its plans for political reforms. Under pressure from the Chinese government and local businessmen, the British agreed to the concept of convergence: whatever Britain did in Hong Kong before 1997 had to converge with China's plans for Hong Kong after 1997. Beijing set up a committee in 1985 to draft the Basic Law or miniconstitution for Hong Kong. That task was to last for five years. In the meantime, the Chinese argued, the British should not make any political changes that might conflict with the provisions of the Basic Law. Britain, by accepting the concept of convergence, gave China the right to veto British decisions, including the holding of direct elections.

Setback for Political Reform

The British had promised to consult the Hong Kong public before proceeding with direct elections. To assess public opinion they therefore set up another institution, known as the Survey Office. The Survey Office commissioned two public opinion surveys. The simple question "Do you favor direct elections in 1988?" was not asked. Instead, the surveys posed a series of questions about the timing of elections, at various levels, and other matters of a technical nature. When the study was completed, the Survey Office reported that the majority of the populace did not support direct elections in 1988. This finding was challenged by professional pollsters, newspaper editorials, political activists and various groups such as the Hong Kong Observers. They pointed out that all other surveys had found a majority of people favoring the introduction of direct elections in 1988. Nevertheless, the government announced in February 1988 that direct elections would not be held until 1991, at which time 10 seats would be selected.

Uncertainty over the future sparked an exodus from Hong Kong. Whereas the normal emigration rate had been about 15,000 a year, it reached 45,000 a year by the late 1980s. Some members of the community called for Britain to restore the citizenship rights of British subjects in Hong Kong, especially the right of abode in the United Kingdom. In the 1960s, Britain had begun to change its immigration laws to abolish the right of certain British subjects to live there. Until that time British subjects around the world had had the same passport that identified them as "Citizen of the United Kingdom and Colonies," with the right to live in Britain. In 1981, Britain created new categories of British nationality, such as British Overseas Citizen and British Dependent Territory Citizen, and issued new passports whose holders would not have the right to live in Britain. That was reserved henceforth for full British citizens. In effect, Britain double-locked its doors.

Few people in Hong Kong had reacted to the earlier immigration-law changes in the 1960s and 1970s, but the nationality-law changes, perceived as designed to exclude Hong Kong British subjects from Britain, provoked a sense of outrage. The cry for a restoration of the right of abode became louder and louder during the 1980s.

Drafting of the Basic Law

With Britain having decided on a pause in Hong Kong's political reforms, China began to devise a constitutional instrument for the future Special Administrative Region. In 1985 China's National People's Congress appointed 59 members to the Basic Law drafting committee. Thirty-six were from the mainland and 23 from Hong Kong.

Chinese officials declared that the Hong Kong public would be fully consulted during the drafting process, and much time was spent soliciting public views. A first draft of the Basic Law was published in April 1988, and the public was consulted in the following months on five topics: the relationship between the central government and the Hong Kong SAR; the fundamental rights and duties of Hong Kong residents; the political structure; the economy; and education, science, culture, sports, religion, labor and social services.

The draft was widely criticized. As was to be expected, the relationship between Hong Kong and the central government in Beijing and the future political structure of Hong Kong received the most attention. This was natural, since both concerned the extent to which Hong Kong would be autonomous. The draft provided for an executive-led government and presented several options for the makeup of the future legislature. Public debate centered on the means of elections, or rather the number of legislators to be directly elected, since there was strong resistance on the part of the conservative business community, as well as from China, to filling all the seats in the legislature through direct elections. Conservative businessmen, then as now, felt that the fewer changes in the status quo, the better. Historically, successful business leaders were automatically appointed by the British to seats on the Legislative and Executive Councils. Democracy presented a potential threat to their political power.

Improvements in Revised Basic Law

In February 1989, a second draft of the Basic Law was released for public consultations. There was general agreement that, aside from the limitations it placed on the number of directly elected seats, the document was significantly improved. The section on human rights, for example, included a provision that restrictions on rights and freedoms must not contravene two major United Nations covenants on human

14

rights—the International Covenant on Civil and Political Rights and its companion, the International Covenant on Economic, Social and Cultural Rights, as applied to Hong Kong. The phrase "as applied to Hong Kong" reflected the fact that Britain had entered certain reservations, such as the right not to hold elections for the Executive Council, when it extended the covenants to Hong Kong in 1976. Such reservations will continue after 1997.

In addition, Chinese laws that would apply to Hong Kong after 1997 were limited to six, listed in an annex. The six laws were largely noncontroversial, dealing with such things as the national anthem, the national emblem, National Day, the territorial sea, diplomatic privileges and nationality.

Another major step forward was the embodiment in the draft Basic Law of an agreement between British and Chinese diplomats to adopt the "through train" formula, so that the last legislators of the British colony could also serve as the first legislators of the Special Administrative Region, with their four-year term straddling 1997 to provide continuity and minimize disruption.

China Playing Dual Role

The Basic Law was thus being shaped in a two-track process, with China sounding out Hong Kong opinion on the one hand and negotiating with Britain on the other. The former process was open, with meetings of the drafting committee covered by the Hong Kong press. The second process was taking place in secrecy.

Despite progress on the drafting of the Basic Law, distrust of the Communist government in Beijing was still pervasive in Hong Kong. Skeptics were convinced the Chinese were not prepared to grant true autonomy to Hong Kong in the crucial areas of political structure and the independence of the judiciary. The draft Basic Law provided for less than half of the legislature to be directly elected; it also concentrated power in the hands of a chief executive who would be appointed by Beijing after "consultations" or "elections" in Hong Kong. In addition, even though the Joint Declaration provided for a court of final appeal in Hong Kong, the Chinese insisted that the right to interpret Hong Kong's Basic Law lay with the Standing Committee of the National People's Congress rather than with the Hong Kong courts.

2

The Tiananmen Massacre
and Its Aftermath

T HE CONSULTATIONS over the second draft of the Basic Law were disrupted by dramatic events in Beijing in May and June 1989, when students took over Tiananmen Square, first to commemorate the death of former Chinese Communist party (CCP) leader Hu Yaobang and later to make demands on the government to curb corruption and inflation and, most importantly, to introduce democracy.

In Hong Kong, groups of students rallied in support of their Beijing counterparts, but the numbers were small at first. That changed radically on May 20, when Beijing proclaimed martial law. On the same day, Hong Kong was struck by a typhoon. As a result, schools and offices were shut, and tens of thousands took to the streets to demonstrate solidarity with the people of Beijing. It was by far the biggest turnout Hong Kong had seen in decades. But that figure was dwarfed in the following days and weeks when more than a million people—almost a fifth of the population—took part in marches and rallies.

A new organization, the Hong Kong Alliance in Support of the Patriotic Democratic Movement in China, was formed. Its leaders were the same people who had spearheaded the democratic movement within Hong Kong. The Hong Kong Alliance, which instantly enjoyed mass support, declared that until China became democratic, there was no hope for Hong Kong to be democratic.

The alliance raised millions of dollars to support the Beijing students, largely through a huge pop-music concert. Tents, blankets and other supplies were sent to Tiananmen Square. Hundreds of thousands of dollars in cash were taken to Beijing. Virtually overnight, a consensus emerged that the colony needed to hasten the development of democracy. On May 25, the *Hongkong Standard* said in an editorial:

> *A week ago it could not have happened. Businessmen and trade unionists, left and right, conservatives and liberals, all agreeing on a political issue. A week ago even the liberals could not agree among themselves. Today, all are united behind Beijing's students, speaking with one voice to condemn the imposition of martial law and, more importantly, to call for the speedier introduction of political reforms in Hong Kong.*

A survey published that same day showed that 92 percent of the population wanted better safeguards for democracy built into the Basic Law. The day before, the noncivil-servant members of both the Executive and Legislative Councils had decided unanimously that the pace of democratization should be speeded up, with 50 percent of the legislature directly elected by 1995, and 100 percent by 2003.

This stance reflected a shift in attitude in Hong Kong society and defiance of China, since the draft Basic Law provided for only 27 percent of the legislature to be directly elected in 1997. Events in Beijing had caused a closing of ranks and a feeling that the development of democracy had to be speeded up, although there were still differences over the rate of speed.

Beijing's imposition of martial law united Hong Kong; the massacre of students and other civilians on June 3–4 created horror and anger. As China moved to impose a news blackout, many in Hong Kong circumvented it. The local radio station began beaming Mandarin-dialect broadcasts to the mainland. People sent newspaper articles by mail and fax to China and circulated videotapes showing the brutality of the massacre. When the Beijing authorities announced lists of wanted student leaders and set up a hot line for the use of informers, people in Hong Kong tried to jam the line by repeatedly calling the number. Some helped create an underground railroad for those on Beijing's wanted list. They managed to spirit out dozens of political dissidents, including the student leader Wu'er Kaixi and political scientist Yan Jiaqi.

While a brave few were helping Chinese dissidents find safe havens, the majority of people in Hong Kong were seized with fear, bordering on panic. Wild schemes gained currency, such as having China lease Hong Kong to the UN for 100 years or recreating Hong Kong in northern Australia. The day after Singapore announced it would accept 25,000 Hong Kong families in the next five to eight years, more than 100,000 people mobbed the Singapore Commission seeking application forms.

Sea Change in China's Attitude toward Hong Kong

China brought pressure to bear on the Hong Kong government to ban the Hong Kong Alliance and to prevent the use of the territory as a base for subverting the Chinese government. Some community leaders called on the Hong Kong Alliance to disband on the ground that it was fueling Chinese anger. The government refused to ban it but agreed Hong Kong would not be a base for subversion.

Chen Xitong, the mayor of Beijing, criticized Hong Kong's role in the pro-democracy uprising in a report to the National People's Congress. He pointed out that supporters in Hong Kong had supplied tents, enabling the students to "set up 'villages of freedom' and launch a 'democracy university' on the square." A few days earlier, on July 11, Jiang Zemin, the new CCP chief, had declared to three Hong Kong visitors, "We practice our socialism and you may practice your capitalism. 'The well water does not interfere with the river water.' We will not practice socialism in Hong Kong, Macao and Taiwan, but you should not transplant capitalism onto the country's mainland."

Jiang used the well-water and river-water metaphor to explain Beijing's "one country, two systems" policy. The price to pay for China's not interfering in Hong Kong affairs, Jiang warned, was for Hong Kong not to meddle in mainland politics. This sounded reasonable enough, but some critics in Hong Kong felt that China did not apply the policy in an evenhanded manner: while Beijing warned Hong Kong not to support democracy on the mainland, it felt no compunction about opposing democracy in Hong Kong. Some in Hong Kong also pointed out that Chinese citizens in Hong Kong had a right to participate in their country's affairs.

In July the official CCP newspaper in Beijing, the *People's Daily*, published an article condemning "a small handful of people in Hong Kong." It criticized the chairman and vice chairman of the Hong Kong Alliance, Szeto Wah and Martin Lee, and—without mentioning their names—accused them and others of "undertaking all sorts of activities to subvert the Chinese government. . . . According to recent press reports," the article continued, "this handful of people is preparing to set up a so-called political party. The 'one country, two systems' principle will certainly be sabotaged and Hong Kong will be in deep trouble once these people gain power."

Hong Kong's corrupting influence on China's cadres was reflected in the fact that even Chinese officials in Hong Kong had joined the pro-democracy protests. These included employees of official Chinese organizations in Hong Kong such as the New China News Agency and the Bank of China. Even Xu Jiatun, China's chief representative in Hong Kong, met and spoke solicitously with Hong Kong hunger strikers.

China moved quickly to restore control over its agents in Hong Kong. Li Tse-chung, director of the *Wen Wei Po* newspaper, who had been a supporter of the Communist cause for four decades, was fired. With that act China revealed for the first time that it controlled the pro-Communist newspapers in

Hong Kong. Previously, it had maintained the polite fiction that they were run by local "patriots." China also sent a new representative to Hong Kong, hard-liner Zhou Nan. Xu Jiatun fled to the United States. From then on, Communist leaders in China began to view Hong Kong as a threat to their country's very survival. This fear was exacerbated after the demise of communism in Europe in 1989–90 and the breakup of the Soviet Union in 1991.

On a practical level, the Tiananmen Square protests and their aftermath led the Chinese leaders to introduce a new article into the Basic Law to curb what they saw as dangerous Hong Kong tendencies. This provision, Article 23, says:

The Hong Kong Special Administrative Region shall enact laws on its own to prohibit any act of treason, secession, sedition, subversion against the Central People's Government, or theft of state secrets, to prohibit foreign political organizations or bodies from conducting political activities in the region, and to prohibit political organizations or bodies of the region from establishing ties with foreign political organizations or bodies.

Britain Reassesses Its Policy

Tiananmen Square also disrupted relations between China and Britain. The British began to change their position on two key issues: nationality and democracy. In July 1989, the foreign secretary, Sir Geoffrey Howe, told the House of Commons that Britain would try to convince China to take steps to boost confidence in Hong Kong, such as refraining from stationing the People's Liberation Army in the territory, delaying the promulgation of the Basic Law and improving its provisions. More importantly, he promised to step up the development of representative government and devise a nationality package to give key people in Hong Kong the confidence to remain there up to and, it was hoped, beyond 1997.

At the same time, Britain sought to bolster international support for its position on Hong Kong. Prime Minister Thatcher brought up the Hong Kong issue in major international forums, including the European summit in Madrid, Spain, the Group of Seven economic summit in Paris and the Commonwealth heads-of-government meeting in Kuala Lumpur, Malaysia. This incurred the wrath of China, which accused the British of "internationalization" of the Hong Kong issue. On September 1, 1989, the *People's Daily* published an article that warned against Hong Kong's pinning its hopes for the future on foreign powers. Two months later the theme was taken up again, with the *People's Daily* claiming that British attempts to garner international support were a violation of international law and a breach of the Joint Declaration. It said that Britain was trying to use international pressure to thwart China's efforts to resume sovereignty over Hong Kong.

In December 1989 Britain unveiled its nationality package. This offered full British nationality to 50,000 key people and their families, a maximum of 225,000 people, in the hope that such an "insurance policy" would, in the words of the new foreign secretary, Douglas Hurd, "anchor them in Hong Kong." About one third of the passports would go to the civil service and two thirds to the private sector.

China denounced the move, claiming that it violated the Joint Declaration. In retaliation, China introduced a provision into the draft Basic Law limiting the number of seats that legislators who held foreign passports or who had the right to live in foreign countries could hold to no more than 15 percent of the total. Chinese officials said they would not recognize such passport holders as foreign nationals and would deny them British consular protection after 1997.

In January 1990, Hurd visited Hong Kong for the first time as foreign secretary. He promised that Britain would soon unveil its plans for representative government but did not promise to adopt the recommendation of Hong Kong's Executive and Legislative Councils, which called for 30 seats to be directly elected by 1997; China's drafting committee proposed 18. Hurd made clear that London's objective was to reach an agreement with Beijing but, failing that, Britain would make its own decisions. Time was running out, as the Chinese time-

Hong Kong's No. 2 official, Chief Secretary Anson Chan, principal adviser to the governor and chief executive of the government. She is the first Chinese and the first woman to hold the position.

table called for the Basic Law to be completed in February and promulgated by the National People's Congress in the spring.

On February 16, 1990, the four-and-a-half-year-long process of drafting the Basic Law came to an end. The day before the drafting committee adopted the final draft, it approved an amendment providing for 20 seats in the legislature to be directly elected in 1997, a reflection of an agreement reached between Britain and China. Minutes after the package was approved, the Hong Kong government announced that 18 seats would be open for direct elections in 1991 and "not less than 20" in 1995. China also agreed to increase to 20 percent the number of legislators who could be foreigners or Chinese who have a right of abode overseas.

In London, Foreign Secretary Hurd told the House of Commons that although the rate of democratization "would not be as rapid as many people in Hong Kong, or we ourselves, would have liked to see...it would be a considerable improvement on the position reached in December."

In another move to restore confidence and to project an image of a government in charge that had a vision of the future, Hong Kong's governor, Sir David Wilson, in his annual address to the legislature on October 11, 1989, unveiled a plan for enhancing Hong Kong's prosperity. The plan included the construction of a new airport on the island of Lantau, capable of handling 80 million passengers a year, or more than three times the capacity of the existing Kai Tak Airport, with the first of two runways to open by early 1997. This would entail building a high-speed rail system, a six-lane highway, and a new town for at least 150,000 people. At the same time, the governor outlined plans for a new port that would increase container throughput fivefold. With 80 million tons of cargo a year, Hong Kong is already the world's busiest container port. The cost of these projects was estimated at HK $127 billion, or U.S. $16.3 billion. Wilson said the government hoped that the private sector could provide 40 to 60 percent of the financing.

What began as a confidence-building measure ended up having the opposite effect. By spring 1990 the airport development plan had turned into a major bone of contention between Hong Kong and China. Banks were reluctant to help finance the project without clear Chinese endorsement, and China made plain its reluctance to support the project without first being fully informed about it. Some Chinese suspected that Britain was using the airport plan to drain the coffers of the reserve that it had agreed to leave behind. The Chinese asked the Hong Kong government for studies done by consultants on the airport project. This seemingly reasonable request was seen by some in Hong Kong as the thin end of the wedge by which China would gradually insinuate itself into Hong Kong's decisionmaking process well before 1997.

The suspicion turned out to be well-founded. China's intention to be fully involved in the administration of Hong Kong became explicit on April 27, 1990. Guo Fengmin, the new Chinese head of the Sino-British Joint Liaison Group set up in 1985 to handle transitional issues, told a press conference that China expected to be consulted on all major decisions involving Hong Kong before 1997.

After long and contentious negotiations, the British agreed to give China a voice in the airport project. A memorandum of understanding was signed in Beijing by Prime Minister John

Major and Premier Li Peng in September 1991. From China's viewpoint, the most important thing about the agreement had nothing to do with the airport: Major's visit was the first to China by the leader of a major Western country since Tiananmen Square. China was still an international pariah at the time, but skillful Chinese negotiators used the Hong Kong airport project to lure the British prime minister to Beijing. The prime minister was clearly uncomfortable posing for pictures with Premier Li Peng. Soon after this visit, the British announced the removal of Wilson as the governor of Hong Kong.

The airport agreement was widely seen as establishing a new and more amicable relationship between China and Britain in the second half of the transitional period, with the British agreeing to consult China on matters that straddle 1997.

3

Transition Years: 1991–96

THE HONG KONG government conducted the first direct elections to the Legislative Council in the colony's 150-year history in September 1991. Much of the campaign hinged on the candidates' attitude toward the Communist government in Beijing. With the memory of the June 3–4 crackdown on pro-democracy students in Tiananmen Square still fresh in voters' minds, the liberals, led by the United Democrats of Hong Kong, with Martin Lee as chairman, garnered the most votes. All pro-China candidates were defeated. Chinese officials, clearly unhappy, did not disavow the election results but pointed to the low turnout. They refused to recognize the Legislative Council, claiming it was merely an advisory body.

The United Democrats urged the governor, in exercising his power of appointment, to bring more liberals into the Legislative Council as a sign that he accepted the will of the people. Sir David, however, selected 18 people who were, on the whole, more conservative than those who had been directly elected and who did not have an overtly political background. Many had served on various government advisory boards and committees. Moreover, the governor declined to appoint any Democrats to the policymaking Executive Council, appointing conservative politicians instead.

Court of Final Appeal

This newly assertive legislature learned soon after it came into being that Britain and China had reached agreement on setting up a court of final appeal. Such a court had been provided for by the Joint Declaration, since Hong Kong's links to the Privy Council in London would be severed in 1997. The Joint Declaration's relevant passage says:

"The power of final judgment of the Hong Kong Special Administrative Region shall be vested in the court of final appeal in the Hong Kong SAR, which may as required invite judges from other common law jurisdictions to sit on the court of final appeal." Almost identical language appears in the Basic Law.

The provision that overseas judges could sit on the court of final appeal was unusual. When China acceded to this in 1984, it was widely seen as a guarantee of the continued independence of the judiciary after 1997, since overseas judges were thought likely to be less susceptible to Chinese political pressure. British and Hong Kong officials also wanted the territory to be able to invite renowned foreign jurists to serve on this Hong Kong court to give it a standing akin to that of the Privy Council. China's acquiescence was seen as a welcome sign of pragmatism and of its willingness to make accommodations where necessary to ensure Hong Kong's prosperity and stability after 1997.

The British sought China's consent to set up the court well before 1997 so that it could gain experience and establish its reputation and authority. In the discussions that began in 1988 the British proposed a five-judge court. Three of the five judges were to be local and the other two, invited overseas judges. The Chinese demurred. The stalemate continued until 1991 when the British and Chinese reached an agreement: the court would comprise five judges, only one of whom could be an overseas judge.

News of the accord triggered an outcry in Hong Kong. Both the Bar Association and the Law Society asserted the agreement "denies the spirit and letter of the Joint Declaration" and "damages the real and perceived independence of the court of final appeal and therefore the judiciary as a whole." Sir William Wade, one of the foremost constitutional-law specialists in the UK, went even further. In his opinion, the power to invite overseas judges "is categorically granted to the court of final appeal by the Basic Law, Article 82, which cannot be altered by an intergovernmental agreement or by any local law of Hong Kong."

Armed with such legal arguments, the newly elected Legislative Council adopted a motion that called for new talks between Britain and China. It was the first time since the Sino-British negotiations had begun almost a decade before that Hong Kong had voted in effect to reject a Sino-British agreement. The Hong Kong government did not implement the agreement, realizing that any legislation was likely to be rejected by the Legislative Council.

There were desultory negotiations on the issue, and it was not until June 1995 that a second agreement was reached. Under that agreement, the composition of the court remained unchanged, with no more than one overseas judge sitting at any one time. The court was to be established before June 30, 1997, as the British wanted, but it would not begin to sit until after July 1, 1997. Chinese appointees, not British ones, would set up the court.

The court would have no jurisdiction "over acts of state such as defense and foreign affairs," as provided in the Basic Law. The problem hinges on the words "such as." There is apprehension that China will interpret "acts of state" widely, and not allow the court jurisdiction even over acts that may be primarily commercial or political in nature.

The business community and foreign governments welcomed the agreement, but the legal community was divided. The Bar Association continued to oppose it, but the Law Society, which represents the solicitors' branch of the legal profession, asserted that it no longer considered the agreement in violation of the Basic Law. The Legislative Council, after a heated debate, voted to uphold the agreement.

British Policy: New Broom

The retirement of Governor Wilson was disclosed in the New Year's honors list, when he was made a member of the House of Lords. The move was widely interpreted in Hong Kong as signaling the advent of a new era when British policy toward China would become more assertive. However, the British government did not decide on a successor until after the general election in April 1992. Then it was announced that Mr. Christopher Patten, the Conservative party chairman who had run the Tories' successful election campaign but who had lost his own seat in Bath, had accepted the governorship of Hong Kong.

Signs of a shift in British policy, or at least a shift in emphasis, soon emerged. The governor-designate, at his first press conference in London, referred to the preservation not only of Hong Kong's prosperity and stability, but of its *"freedom,* prosperity and stability" (emphasis added). He indicated he might make some changes in Hong Kong after his arrival and that he was coming with a fresh eye and an open mind. He declined to wear the colonial gubernatorial uniform, complete with plumed hat, at his inauguration. It was also disclosed that he would take the oath of office as simply Mr. Chris Patten—the first governor in Hong Kong's history not to arrive as a knight of the realm. Mr. Patten also strongly suggested that Democrats would be appointed to the Executive Council.

This stirred up controversy even before Patten's arrival. Chinese official Guo Fengmin made his government's position on the issue very clear. "We are of the view that the admission of those people who are against the Basic Law and openly propagate subversion against the legitimate government of China will not be conducive to the stability of Hong Kong. Therefore we oppose this."

Meanwhile, there was renewed controversy over the proposed airport. The memorandum of 1991 provided that Hong Kong had to consult China on such issues as financing, and that the Chinese had to respond within a month. By late spring, Hong Kong had been unable to get China to agree to the financing arrangements for the new airport. When Prime Minister Major met Premier Li at the Earth Summit in Rio de Janeiro, Brazil, in June 1992, the two men agreed to hold high-level talks to resolve the impasse.

By the end of June 1992, however, disagreements over appointments to the Executive Council overshadowed the dispute over the proposed airport. China justified its insistence on a veto by saying, through Ambassador Guo, that during the transitional period, "all important issues should be discussed with us. There needs to be convergence with the Basic Law. There should be discussion on important issues."

Patten Politics

Patten's arrival in July ushered in a new era of politics in Hong Kong. A politician down to his fingertips, the new governor and his family took Hong Kong by storm. His informality quickly won him acceptance in Hong Kong. He sometimes acted as though he were campaigning, kissing babies and hugging children. (One Chinese official upbraided the governor, reminding him that he was not running for office in Hong Kong.)

The new governor wanted to institute change, but he did not have a free hand. A decade of negotiations between Britain and China had resulted in numerous agreements that could not be easily undone. In particular, the Basic Law that the National People's Congress of China had promulgated in April 1990 stipulated how Hong Kong's post-1997 legislature would be constituted. Patten knew, although the Hong Kong public did not, that even before the Basic Law was adopted the British government had indicated to Beijing its acceptance of limitations on democratic development.

Britain's governor of Hong Kong since 1992, Chris Patten, fielded questions at 10 Downing Street, London, following a meeting with Prime Minister John Major on Hong Kong 1997.

Thus, the governor's room for maneuver was limited. He spent the first three months meeting people and getting a better feel for Hong Kong. He avoided making policy statements and promised to disclose his position on key issues when he delivered the annual address to the legislature in October 1992. The members of the Executive Council, in the meantime, offered to resign to allow the new governor to pick his own advisers. Patten called it "a generous offer" but did not indicate whether he would accept it.

In October, Governor Patten did accept the resignations from the Executive Council of all four members of the conservative grouping known as the Cooperative Resources Center— Allen Lee, Selina Chow, Edward Ho and Rita Fan. At the same time, he announced a new policy: henceforth no one could serve on the Executive and Legislative Councils at the same time. This was Patten's way of justifying not appointing Democrats to the Executive Council without seeming to be giving in to Chinese demands. The severance of ties between the Executive and the Legislative Councils was presented as a move toward greater separation of powers between the two branches of government. However, since the legislature was at least partially elected, ending dual membership meant that the Executive Council became a body with no elected members. It thus became less accountable and somewhat more isolated from the political process.

Patten's Democracy Package

In his October address to the legislature, the governor unveiled his proposals for greater democracy in Hong Kong. The Basic Law provides for a 60-seat legislature in 1997, with 20 seats filled by direct elections, 30 by functional constituencies and 10 by an election committee. While technically adhering to the Basic Law's stipulations, the governor widened the franchise significantly by proposing that every working person should have a vote in a functional constituency. He did this by creating nine new functional constituencies, which embraced the entire work force. The original functional constituencies were largely elitist bodies. The effect was to make these nine seats scarcely distinguishable from the 20 directly elected seats. He also proposed the total phasing out of appointments to the lowest tier of government, the district boards, and that the election committee be made up of directly elected district board members.

The rest of the Patten package had to do with such things as lowering the voting age from 21 to 18 and widening the franchise in some of the existing 21 functional constituencies. But the most controversial proposals were the ones relating to the nine new functional constituencies and the makeup of the election committee. These were widely seen as a thinly disguised attempt to increase the number of democratically elected legislators from the 20 laid down in the Basic Law to a total of 39.

Immediately after announcing his proposals, the governor engaged in a whirlwind of activities to explain them to the public and to win support. He held an unprecedented series of town hall meetings, where anyone could attend and ask him questions. He went on radio call-in programs. He appeared on television to answer questions from a panel, including hostile questioners such as the editor of the pro-Communist newspaper *Wen Wei Po* and James Tien, a former appointee of the Wilson era.

Patten made himself accessible in a way that no governor had ever done before. In addition to giving an incredible number of interviews to both the print and electronic media, local and overseas, he met with representatives of political groups, some of whom told him he had gone too far, while others said he had not gone far enough. The governor himself insisted that he had found a "point of balance" that was just about right.

Patten instituted a governor's "Question Time" in the Legislative Council, when he would answer any questions that legislators might wish to ask him. This became a monthly affair. The governor also gave up the presidency of the Legislative Council. This position was filled by John Swaine, who had previously served as acting president. Swaine became the first legislator to preside over the chamber.

Beijing Rebuffs Patten

The public's initial response to the governor's proposals was overwhelmingly positive. He appeared to have found a way to satisfy demands for greater democracy while remaining within the confines of the Basic Law. But this situation soon changed. When the governor went to Beijing to explain his proposals, he was snubbed: not a single senior member of the leadership granted him an audience. His meetings with Lu Ping, director of the Hong Kong and Macao Affairs Office under the State Council, did not go well. In fact, within minutes of the governor's departure from Beijing, Lu held a press conference in which he denounced the governor's proposals and threatened that China would, if necessary, "build a second stove," that is, create its own governmental structure for Hong Kong. He also said that if the British went ahead and built the new airport without Chinese approval, planes using that airport would not be allowed to fly to China. This was a strange threat since the airport was not scheduled to be completed until Hong Kong became part of China.

Lu and other Chinese officials were careful to focus their attacks on Patten in the hope of driving a wedge between him and the British government in London. The governor publicly declared that he and British Prime Minister Major were so close that there was not even room to put a piece of tissue paper between them. In the event, the governor continued to enjoy the support of both the prime minister and Foreign Secretary Hurd, even after the disclosure of an embarrassing series of letters that Hurd had exchanged with his Chinese counterpart, Foreign Minister Qian Qichen.

The Chinese revealed that, in addition to the Joint Declaration and the Basic Law, London and Beijing had reached "other relevant agreements and understandings" regarding Hong Kong that had to be honored. An outcry arose in Hong Kong calling for the letters to be made public. Eventually seven letters, exchanged in early 1990 before the final adoption of the Basic Law, were released. They showed that, contrary to the public position of Britain that it had pressed China to give Hong Kong as much democracy as possible, the British actually had asked for much less than Hong Kong wanted, and eventually settled for even less than that. Instead of insisting that 30 seats, or 50 percent of the legislature, be directly elected in 1995, Hurd, at least by early 1990, was asking for only 24 seats to be directly elected in 1995. He ultimately settled for 20 seats. This was then incorporated in the Basic Law.

In the letters, Hurd also said he agreed "in principle" that the Basic Law's provision for the election committee would be put into effect in Hong Kong in 1995 rather than 1999. It therefore appeared to the Chinese that Patten was reneging on the previous understanding.

34

Political Repercussions in Hong Kong

The Patten proposals had a curious effect on the political groupings in Hong Kong. The United Democrats, who during the Wilson era were firmly in the opposition, warmed to Patten. While saying that he did not go far enough, the Democrats were pleased by his reform plans. But the Cooperative Resources Center, which during the Wilson era was strongly progovernment, in effect turned into an opposition party. A change in Britain's attitudes toward China had resulted in a reversal of roles on the part of the two major political groupings in Hong Kong.

This period also saw a strong surge in the development of political parties. A pro-Beijing party, the Democratic Alliance for the Betterment of Hong Kong, was inaugurated the day after Patten's arrival in Hong Kong. Its chairman was Tsang Yok-sing, principal of what used to be known as a "patriotic" school. The party's 56 founding members included Vice Chairman Tam Yiu-chung, a serving legislator, as well as Cheng Kai-nam and Chan Yuen-han, candidates in the 1991 Legislative Council elections who had lost their bid for seats.

The new party issued a strong warning against outside interference in Hong Kong's political affairs. Tsang described the party as both "pro-China and pro-Hong Kong." He said: "We support China's policy toward Hong Kong. But such a stand would never stop us from serving Hong Kong's interest."

Meanwhile, the Cooperative Resources Center was trying to turn itself into a political party. The situation was unusual because all the members of the group were legislators; the leader was an appointed member, Allen Lee. The group had little grass-roots support; an opinion survey published in August 1992 showed that only 11 percent of the public supported it, 24 points behind the United Democrats. The total support for liberal groups, including Meeting Point and the Association for Democracy and People's Livelihood, stood at 49 percent, while that of conservative and pro-Beijing groups was 20 percent.

The United Democrats, formed in April 1990, was by far the largest of the liberal groupings, with 600 members. However, because the principal leaders and the group itself had in effect been blacklisted by Chinese officials, it had great difficulty in expanding its membership and raising funds. Chinese officials in Beijing and with the New China News Agency in Hong Kong rebuffed the United Democrats' efforts to open a dialogue.

The United Democrats' dilemma was that if they stayed on a confrontational course with Beijing, they would continue to be ostracized by people fearful of bringing down China's wrath on Hong Kong. On the other hand, a conciliatory attitude toward Beijing would risk charges that the group was abandoning its principles and result in an erosion of its core supporters. Beijing's perception of the group as anti-China was strengthened by the fact that many of the party's leaders, such as Martin Lee and Szeto Wah, were also leaders of the Hong Kong Alliance. The party constantly found itself torn between wanting to support the more assertive British line represented by Governor Patten, fear of being branded a pro-government party, and a natural inclination to go even further than the Patten proposals.

By 1993 three liberal groups—the United Democrats, Meeting Point and the Association for Democracy and People's Livelihood—were holding sporadic meetings in an attempt to reach consensus. Ultimately, the first two groups merged and formed a new entity, the Democratic party, with Martin Lee as chairman. China immediately made known its opposition to the party and withdrew the appointment of Anthony Cheung, the head of Meeting Point, as adviser on Hong Kong affairs. Meanwhile, the conservative, pro-business Cooperative Resources Center had metamorphosed into the Liberal party.

The 'Second Stove': Preliminary Working Committee

Chinese officials in February 1993 renewed their threat to set up a "second stove" in Hong Kong if the British insisted on going their own way. They made good the threat in July when they established a new body with the unwieldy title of the

Preliminary Working Committee of the Preparatory Committee of the Hong Kong Special Administrative Region. The chairman was Qian Qichen, China's vice-premier and foreign minister. By creating the Preliminary Working Committee in 1993, China was moving up its schedule to prepare for the takeover of Hong Kong by three years. Instead of counting on British cooperation, China had decided, in the words of Qian Qichen, to adopt a policy of "using ourselves as the mainstay."

China refused at first even to discuss the Patten proposals but, after months of talks about talks, ultimately agreed to formal negotiations. However, after seven months of wrangling, the British announced at the end of 1993 that time was running out. Patten's reform proposals would be presented to the legislature, and it would be up to the Legislative Council to decide whether to accept them. In a marathon session that went on until 2:30 in the morning, the Legislative Council approved the electoral proposals and passed them into law on June 30, 1994. Britain and China were going their separate ways.

Sino-British Differences Harden

By and large, 1994 was marked by serious quarrels between Britain and China. One of the few accords reached was over the handling of military property in Hong Kong. The British promised to turn over all land held by the British military to China's People's Liberation Army. The Chinese agreed that the land would not be used for commercial purposes and, if no longer required by the Chinese garrison, would be turned over to the Hong Kong government.

The principal quarrel was over the Patten reforms. The Chinese made it clear that they would not be bound by them, and on August 31, 1994, the Standing Committee of China's National People's Congress passed a resolution declaring that the terms of office of Hong Kong's three tiers of elected bodies—district boards, municipal councils and the legislature—would terminate on June 30, 1997.

The Chinese subsequently revealed that the Legislative Council, to be elected in September 1995, would be replaced by a provisional legislature on July 1, 1997. This announcement provoked great controversy in Hong Kong since there was no provision in the Basic Law for such a body. By calling the first legislature the Provisional Legislature, the Chinese sought to free themselves of the need to follow the Basic Law's prescriptions. It was unclear how the members of the Provisional Legislature would be elected, or whether they would be elected at all.

Bill of Rights

The Preliminary Working Committee further alarmed Hong Kong by proposing to delete two key sections from the bill of rights: one provides for repeal of all existing legislation that is not consistent with the bill of rights; the other prohibits the introduction of new legislation that is inconsistent with the bill of rights. The removal of these two sections would emasculate the bill of rights.

In support of their position, the Preliminary Working Committee cited previous British policy. Britain had informed the UN in 1978 that the rights set out in the International Covenant on Civil and Political Rights were protected by "safeguards of different kinds operating...independently of the covenant but in full conformity with it." Since all rights were fully protected by existing legislation and existing legislation was fully consistent with the covenant, there was no need for a bill of rights. The British maintained this position until the early 1990s. After Tiananmen, Britain reversed itself and enacted the Bill of Rights Ordinance.

In addition to urging the watering down of the bill of rights itself, the Preliminary Working Committee called for the restoration of some of the dozens of draconian laws that had been repealed or amended after Patten's arrival because they were found to be in conflict with the bill of rights. The Chinese argued that the British had needed those laws to administer Hong Kong and, now that they were leaving, they were

The UN and Human Rights

The British government submits reports periodically to the UN on the human-rights situation in Hong Kong. China is not a signatory of the two UN human-rights covenants and, even though it agreed in the Joint Declaration and the Basic Law that the two covenants would continue to apply to Hong Kong after 1997, it denies that it is under any obligation to report to the UN. Nor will China let Hong Kong report directly to the UN because, it points out, only states can be signatories to the covenants and Hong Kong is not a state.

The UN Human Rights Committee, in an unusual move, stated its view that "once the people living in a territory find themselves under the protection of the International Covenant on Civil and Political Rights, such protection cannot be denied to them by virtue of the mere dismemberment of that territory or its coming within the jurisdiction of another state or of more than one state."

The committee went on to say that Article 40 of the covenant provides that human-rights reports shall be submitted periodically to the committee. "As the reporting requirements will continue to apply," the committee said, "the Human Rights Committee considers that it is competent to receive and review reports that must be submitted in relation to Hong Kong." In other words, the committee pronounced itself willing to receive reports on Hong Kong either from China, which is not a signatory, or from Hong Kong, which is not a state. But the Chinese remain adamant. It appears, therefore, that the UN will be unable to maintain its current role of monitoring the human-rights situation in Hong Kong after the change in sovereignty.

creating trouble for the new Special Administrative Region government by depriving it of the tools necessary to run Hong Kong.

The Elections of 1995

The much-debated Patten reform proposals were implemented in September 1995, when the last elections under British sovereignty were held. The Democrats' expectations were low. In 1991, the Democrats were thought to have benefited from the backlash against the Tiananmen Square massacre. This time around, the thinking went, voters would choose people who had a less confrontational attitude toward China.

The results, however, showed that support for the Democrats had not slipped. The party won the most seats—19. By contrast, three of the four leaders of the pro-Beijing party, the Democratic Alliance for the Betterment of Hong Kong, were defeated, although a number of its lesser known candidates did win seats. The outcome was seen as a strong affirmation by the people of Hong Kong of their desire to maintain their way of life and to preserve their rights and freedoms.

In fact, the media, including the overseas press, exaggerated the magnitude of the Democratic victory, largely because the party's expectations had been so low. The party actually did little better than in 1991, when it ran as the United Democrats. Part of the reason for the Democrats' success was their ability to field incumbents, all of whom were reelected. The only incumbents who lost were defeated by other incumbents. The Democrats won the most seats because they had the largest number of incumbents running.

The pro-business Liberal party came in second, with 10 seats, a drop from 15. All those who won were incumbents, and all new Liberal party candidates were defeated, a fact that did not bode well for the party's future.

As for the pro-China party, despite the defeat of its stars, it did surprisingly well, increasing its representation in the legislature from one seat to six. The number of votes it received was comparable to that received by Democratic candidates, though it won far fewer seats. From this it would appear that many Hong Kong voters found pro-China candidates acceptable. They are likely to do even better after 1997, whereas the Democrats' fortunes are expected to fall.

4

Hong Kong's Economy

HONG KONG, which is not only a principal gateway to China but also a hub for the Asia-Pacific region, has shared in the rapid economic growth of the East Asia region. It has experienced 35 years of economic expansion, most dramatically during the last decade. Per capita income in Hong Kong is now even higher than in Canada, Australia and Britain.

Hong Kong's economic success is attributable to various factors, including its geographical location on China's doorstep. Created in the 19th century to facilitate trade between the West and China, it continues to play that role.

Moreover, its location midway between Tokyo and Singapore has enabled it to become a business hub. Efficient transportation and communications infrastructures make it easy for businessmen to travel to almost anywhere in the world, or to any of the major capitals in the region.

Hong Kong also has a well-educated and hardworking labor

Hong Kong 1995 Indicators

	Population	**6.3 million**
	Gross Domestic Product ($U.S.)	**149.0 billion**
	Real GDP Growth Rate	**5.0%**
	GDP Per Capita ($U.S.)	**24,100**
	Inflation	**8.7%**
	Unemployment	**3.5%**
	Hong Kong-U.S. Trade ($U.S.)	**18.2 billion**
	Hong Kong-China Trade ($U.S.)	**127.6 billion***

* includes $U.S. 49.7 billion of reexports

Robert Mansfield

force. Part of its legacy as a British colony is a large number of English-speaking people whose language skills enhance the value of the territory. Mandarin, the official national language of China, is also widely understood, so Hong Kong is well positioned to act as a crossroads for China and the rest of the world.

The territory also benefits from a large number of entrepreneurial businessmen who are constantly on the lookout for new opportunities. It boasts a level playing field for business, as well as an efficient, honest and apolitical civil service and an independent judiciary.

As a result of all these factors, Hong Kong has now developed into the eighth-largest trading entity in the world. In fact, if the European Union is counted as a single entity, then tiny Hong Kong is the world's fourth-largest trading entity. It is also the fifth-largest financial center in terms of both external-banking transactions and foreign-exchange transactions, with over 500 foreign banking institutions from more than 40 countries located there.

According to a conservative appraisal by the Heritage Foundation, a Washington-based research organization, Hong Kong is the world's freest economy and, according to the *World Competitiveness Report 1995*, published by the Geneva-based World Economic Forum, Hong Kong is the third-most-competitive economy in the world. In addition, it has the world's busiest container port, the world's third-busiest airport in terms of international passenger throughput and the eighth-largest stock market in the world in terms of capitalization.

The 6.3 million people of Hong Kong account for 21 percent of the gross domestic product (GDP) of China, a nation of 1.2 billion people. And Hong Kong is responsible for about 65 percent of the external investment in China.

Hong Kong taxes are low. The highest tax on salaries is 15 percent, and that is paid by only 2 percent of the work force. Corporations pay no more than 16.5 percent of profits in taxes. Public spending has remained at less than 20 percent of GDP. The Hong Kong currency will be maintained after 1997, and will continue to be convertible, regardless of the state of the renminbi, China's currency.

Notwithstanding the generally favorable picture, the Hong Kong economy in the latter half of 1995 was in the doldrums. The unemployment rate soared to 3.5 percent, the highest level in over a decade. To a large extent, this reflected the restructuring of the Hong Kong economy that had been taking place in the decade since the signing of the Joint Declaration.

In the early 1980s, when Britain and China were negotiating the future of Hong Kong, the territory's economy was largely based on manufacturing. However, as China continued its open-door policy, more and more Hong Kong manufactures shifted production lines across the border into Guangdong province to take advantage of the cheaper labor available there. By the mid-1990s, the Hong Kong and Chinese economies had become so integrated that Hong Kong manufacturers employed several million workers within

China, or more than the total number of workers within Hong Kong itself.

Manufacturing no longer provides many jobs in Hong Kong, which is being transformed into a service economy, focusing on such areas as tourism, banking, shipping and transportation. Over 80 percent of the territory's GDP now comes from services, and about 70 percent of the work force is employed in that sector.

In part because of rising unemployment, the government has been increasing its social-service expenditures on the elderly, the disabled and other less fortunate members of society. This has aroused China's suspicions, and a senior Chinese official pointedly warned that Hong Kong appeared in danger of spending beyond its means. The charge appears groundless: Hong Kong's reserves are sound. While Britain has agreed to leave HK $25 billion in the reserves on June 30, 1997, estimates suggest that the incoming Special Administrative Region government will have in excess of HK $365 billion in its kitty when it takes over on July 1.

The business community by and large tends to be conservative and, in the quarrel between China and Governor Patten on democratic reforms, has tended to support China rather than Patten. This was true to such an extent that the governor, during his much publicized visit to Canada and the United States in May 1996, accused wealthy businessmen of betraying Hong Kong for their own benefit.

Such charges were vehemently rejected by, among others, James Tien, chairman of the Hong Kong General Chamber of Commerce. "We may not be overly enthusiastic about Mr. Patten's reforms," Tien wrote, "but that is hardly surprising when holding a belief of the least change the better during a transitional period, which in itself is to usher in the greatest change the territory has known since World War II.

"Instead of selling out the people, we are also the people and we have contributed enormously to the entire territory," he said. "The business sector has generated the wealth which enables our government to provide decent services, improve the quality of life and build impressive infrastructure."

5

Uncertain Future

THE TENSE RELATIONS between Britain and China relaxed somewhat in late 1995, when Chinese Foreign Minister Qian Qichen visited London, a visit reciprocated by Britain's new foreign secretary, Malcolm Rifkind, in January 1996. However, the improved atmosphere did not last long. The main issue remained the Patten reforms, with the British government backing the governor. China's decision to replace the legislature elected in September 1995 with a provisional legislature, a decision Rifkind denounced as "reprehensible and unjustifiable," contributed to the anxious mood in Hong Kong.

The high state of anxiety on the part of Hong Kong's residents became evident in March 1996. The Hong Kong government had announced in 1993 that the deadline for applications for naturalization to become British subjects was March 31, 1996. (As noted earlier, those applicants who are approved will not have the right to live in Britain, but they will get a form of British passport which will entitle them to visa-free entry to

Britain and many other countries. This is expected to be a much more acceptable travel document than the as-yet untested Special Administrative Region passport.)

By mid-March 1996, as the deadline for naturalization applications approached, the street outside the Immigration Department was packed every day with thousands of people, young and old, standing in line to apply for second-class British citizenship. By the end of the month, the Immigration Department had to keep its doors open 24 hours a day to handle the crowds. March 31 was a Sunday, but the department continued to work and only shut its doors at one minute to midnight. That day, more than 54,000 people applied for naturalization to become British, knowing that Britain's sovereignty over Hong Kong would end in 15 months.

In the 12 years since the signing of the Joint Declaration, about 600,000 people have emigrated. Many have returned to Hong Kong with foreign passports, which they see as an insurance policy. Others have left their families in North America while they work in Hong Kong. These people spend so much of their time in the air that they are known locally as astronauts.

To some extent, the applicants were risking the wrath of Beijing, since they would have to swear allegiance to Britain's Queen Elizabeth as well as her heirs and successors before they could be naturalized. But Chinese officials in Hong Kong pretended that these vast queues had nothing to do with a lack of confidence in post-1997 Hong Kong, or in the future SAR passport.

Some of the people who stood in line attributed their anxiety to recent Chinese actions, in particular to what became known as the Frederick Fung affair.

A Single Negative Vote

When the Preparatory Committee voted to replace the legislature with a provisional legislature, China's views on the issue were well known and there was a solitary dissenting vote. That vote was cast by Frederick Fung, chairman of the Association for Democracy and People's Livelihood. The Chinese government made clear its displeasure. Lu Ping, the highest official responsible for implementing China's policy on Hong Kong, denounced Mr. Fung for having supposedly answered Governor Patten's call to oppose the provisional legislature. Mr. Lu said that Mr. Fung would not be allowed to sit on the selection committee, which is to choose the future chief executive and the members of the provisional legislature, nor would he be allowed to sit in the provisional legislature.

The Hong Kong public was taken aback by the severity of China's reaction to a single negative vote in a body of 150 people. It suggested that China would not tolerate any dissent in Hong Kong. Although Mr. Lu said later that he was merely expressing his personal view, it was clear that his words represented much more than that. Mr. Fung himself disclosed that three different Chinese officials had warned him in the days leading up to the vote of the consequences he would suffer if he decided to oppose the provisional legislature.

China's insistence on a provisional legislature suggests that Beijing intends to use it to pass legislation ensuring China's control of Hong Kong. For one thing, there is widespread suspicion that the provisional legislature will create legal impediments to the seating of leaders of the Democratic party. The provisional legislature is also expected to water down Hong Kong's bill of rights and pass new laws restricting freedom of expression, including freedom of speech, freedom of the press and the right to hold public demonstrations.

Recent events have added to the sense of fear and uncertainty. In April 1996, Lu Ping went to Hong Kong on his first visit in almost a year. As was the case in previous visits, he refused to meet with Governor Patten, but he did agree to meet Chief Secretary Anson Chan. The purpose of his trip ostensibly was to consult the Hong Kong public on how to form the selection committee. On this issue, too, China received a bad press.

The Chinese took the position that because the selection committee's job would be to choose not just the chief executive but also the members of the provisional legislature, those who appeared before it to present their views had to support the formation of the provisional legislature, or at least not oppose it. Surprisingly, the Preparatory Committee invited representatives from the Professional Teachers' Union, headed by Cheung Man-kwong and Szeto Wah, both of whom are legislators as well as leaders of the Hong Kong Alliance, to address it.

Before the appointed date, the invitation was suddenly withdrawn, ostensibly because the union had been making public statements opposing the provisional legislature. This was taken as further evidence of China's intolerance. In their place, the Preparatory Committee invited two representatives from a radical student group, the Hong Kong Federation of Students. On April 14, the day of the consultations, the two student representatives were unceremoniously ejected from the room when they distributed leaflets opposing the provisional legislature. This was followed by scuffles between student demonstrators and the police, and a senior Chinese official had to flee the scene by taxi. The Communist-backed *Wen Wei Po* on April 16 published a commentary accusing Governor Patten of orchestrating the protests.

To the credit of the Preparatory Committee, it also invited the Bar Association to offer its views on the selection committee, even though the association's opposition to the provisional legislature was well known. At the end of the two-day consultation period, it was announced that the vast majority of those who appeared had supported the establishment of a provisional legislature.

One Country, One System?

The root problem is that Beijing is unwilling to face up to the consequences of the policy of "one country, two systems." The implication of such a policy is that mainland China will run its affairs without Hong Kong's interference, and that Hong Kong will run its affairs without Beijing's interference. For the policy to work, each system must generate its own leadership.

Hong Kongers line up outside the Immigration Department to get applications for British passports before the cutoff date of March 31, 1996.

AP/Wide World Photos

If the leaders of one system control the leaders of the other system, soon there will not be two systems.

China insists on appointing the future chief executive of Hong Kong and his principal officials. Hong Kong originally understood the appointments to be a formality, but Beijing now says that they are substantive and has even called on the Hong Kong government to provide it with the personnel files of senior officials so Beijing can make its selection. It appears that China also wants to control the legislature. It has sponsored a political party, the Democratic Alliance for the Betterment of Hong Kong, which it supports financially. China has mobilized support for the party's candidates and other pro-China figures by telling people who work for China-funded enterprises to vote for them. Its newspapers in Hong Kong provide favorable publicity for these candidates, while ignoring or denouncing those who do not enjoy China's favor.

The apprehension in Hong Kong has been increased by China's continued refusal to have any dealings with Governor Patten. Although China and Britain agreed in late 1995, during Foreign Minister Qian's visit to London, to mark the handover of the territory on June 30, 1997, with a joint ceremony that would be grand and solemn, the two sides remained deadlocked on details and, in mid-1996, Patten raised the possibility of the two governments holding separate ceremonies.

The business community nevertheless continues to express undiminished confidence in the future. At a conference on April 12, 1996, jointly sponsored by the Hong Kong Trade Development Council and the Better Hong Kong Foundation, major business leaders repeatedly asserted their belief in Hong Kong's future stability and prosperity.

Nationality and Right of Abode

On his most recent visit to Hong Kong, Lu Ping's principal speech dealt with the sensitive topic of nationality and the right of abode in Hong Kong after 1997. He spoke in conciliatory terms, and said that even though China's nationality law did not countenance dual nationality, Hong Kong people would be allowed to travel on foreign passports after the takeover in 1997.

He explained that those who have obtained foreign passports would still be treated as Chinese nationals, even though the nationality law provides that any Chinese citizen who voluntarily acquires foreign nationality through naturalization automatically loses Chinese nationality. Mr. Lu said that as long as these people do not insist on being treated as foreigners, they would be treated as Chinese nationals and would still have the right of abode in Hong Kong. But they would not be accorded consular protection in case of trouble.

However, if possessors of foreign passports insist on being treated as foreigners, he said, they would lose their right of abode in Hong Kong. They could only regain that right after living in Hong Kong for seven more years.

Mr. Lu also introduced the concept of "Chinese blood" without defining it in legal or scientific terms. He said that all Hong Kong residents of Chinese blood who were born in either Hong Kong or China would be considered Chinese nationals, regardless of whether or not they have acquired foreign nationality. This approach is different from that of the nationality law, which requires that at least one parent must be a Chinese national.

Since the Chinese population consists of more than 50 major ethnic groups, it was unclear how this concept would be applied. Moreover, many such groups (Mongols, Koreans and Kazakhs) can be found in countries other than China. And Singapore, of course, consists mainly of people who are ethnic Chinese. It was unclear whether the children of the 8,000 or so Singaporean residents in Hong Kong would in the future be considered Chinese nationals unless they declared themselves foreigners.

Mr. Lu's speech was generally well received, since it appeared to offer the best of both worlds: the right to live in Hong Kong as a Chinese national, along with the right to travel abroad on a foreign passport. Moreover, if things went badly, those who possessed foreign passports would have a place to escape to. But there was some unease that under this concept of "Chinese blood," foreign nationals may be treated as Chinese nationals.

The Future from China's Perspective

China's decision to recover its sovereignty over Hong Kong stemmed from reasons of national honor. Even though the Chinese did not initiate the process that ended with the Sino-British Joint Declaration, once the British forced them to make a decision, they concluded that the most they could do was to permit British rule to continue until July 1, 1997, but they would not permit British administration to continue beyond that date.

Various Chinese officials have referred to China's resumption of sovereignty over Hong Kong as marking the end of a period of humiliation by foreigners, especially by the British. On one level, China continues to see itself engaged in a political struggle with Britain, and it is unwilling to give any ground over political issues. On another level, however, China wants to prevent Hong Kong from being transformed from what it sees as an economic city into what it calls a political city. But the genie is now out of the bottle, and it is difficult to see how the political aspirations of the people of Hong Kong for self-rule can be successfully contained, if indeed that is what China wishes to do.

The man who initiated the concept of "one country, two systems," Deng Xiaoping, is now in his 90s and, by all accounts, no longer physically or mentally able to play any role in the decisionmaking process in China. The man who signed the Joint Declaration with Mrs. Thatcher, Zhao Ziyang, was ousted from office as a result of the Tiananmen Square demonstrations. Yet China's current leaders, President Jiang Zemin and Premier Li Peng, continue to assert that the policy toward Hong Kong remains unchanged. China still hopes to make use of Hong Kong as a conduit for its trade and as a source of capital and management expertise.

And Hong Kong may still remain useful in another way. China wants Taiwan to be reunified with the mainland, and to accept, like Hong Kong, the status of a Special Administrative Region. Although Taiwan has steadfastly rejected this proposal, Beijing must still think if Hong Kong continues to prosper after 1997, the Taiwanese opposition may gradually begin to dissipate.

Taiwan's Future in Hong Kong

While Taiwan wants to have a free hand in Hong Kong after 1997, this is unlikely to happen. China fully intends to keep all official Taiwanese organizations under its control. At a plenary session of the Preliminary Working Committee in June 1995, Vice Premier Qian delivered a major speech in

which he made public China's policies regarding Taiwan's relations with post-1997 Hong Kong. These policies, couched in seven articles, attempt to preserve the economic ties that exist between Hong Kong and Taiwan while drawing the latter into a new political relationship with the mainland in which Beijing would implicitly be acknowledged as the central government, with jurisdiction over the 22 million Taiwanese, despite their leaders' official policy of shunning direct contact.

Thus, according to Qian, official contacts or talks between Taiwan and Hong Kong cannot be held without first being approved by the central government in Beijing. In this way, Taiwan would have to accept the fact that any dealings with Hong Kong would in effect be dealings with the representatives of the Communist government in Beijing.

The Chinese position further specified political conditions that Taiwanese organizations and their staffs would have to meet if they wished to stay in Hong Kong after 1997. According to Qian, they "must abide by the Basic Law and cannot engage in activities which would damage Hong Kong's stability or prosperity." Qian also said that Taiwanese residents would be able to enter and leave Hong Kong, but not by using their Taiwanese passports. Instead, he said, "the central government will make arrangements for necessary documents and other matters."

This change in travel documents for Taiwanese going to Hong Kong is politically significant. For if the people of Taiwan accept travel documents issued by Beijing, they will in effect be acknowledging that they come within the jurisdiction of the People's Republic of China. Passports, after all, are the most common manifestation of a person's nationality and political loyalty.

At present, Taiwan's main official representative body is the Chung Hwa Travel Service, whose managing director has traditionally been Taiwan's de facto representative in Hong Kong. This arrangement is unlikely to continue after 1997. The Chinese policy statement pointedly says that after 1997 Taiwanese organizations in Hong Kong "may not do anything not covered by their registration licenses." This means that if the Chung Hwa Travel Service is registered as a travel service, it will have to confine itself to that particular business and will no longer be able to function as a de facto consulate.

As to who will represent Taiwan's official interests in Hong Kong after 1997, an appropriate body would be the Straits Exchange Foundation, Taiwan's quasi-official body which has been handling negotiations with China's quasi-official body, the Association for Relations Across the Taiwan Straits. Whether China will allow the Taiwan foundation an official presence in Hong Kong is another matter.

Perhaps ironically, Taiwanese President Lee Teng-hui said in May 1995 that Taiwan was determined "to maintain normal contact with Hong Kong" after 1997 and, moreover, that it would work to enhance freedom and democracy in Hong Kong. Qian's statement made it absolutely clear that, in China's view, Taiwan has no business trying to enhance democracy and freedom in Hong Kong. Even maintenance of Taiwan's current contacts won't be possible without the express approval of the Beijing government.

Implications for the U.S.

The United States has had a long and close historical relationship with Hong Kong, which today is its 13th-largest trading partner. The American stake in Hong Kong is also large, with billions of dollars in investments and more than 1,000 companies with offices in Hong Kong. The American Chamber of Commerce in Hong Kong is the largest in the world outside the United States.

Since the Tiananmen Square tragedy, the United States has been concerned about Hong Kong's future after its takeover by China in 1997. Some members of Congress have proposed linking renewal of China's most-favored-nation trading status with its treatment of Hong Kong. China, not unexpectedly, opposes such conditions and has made it clear that after 1997, how it treats Hong Kong will be China's internal affair and Beijing will brook no outside interference.

The United States has taken some special measures to assist Hong Kong. The U.S.-Hong Kong Policy Act, sponsored by Senator Mitch McConnell Jr. (R-Ky.) in 1992, provides strong American support for Hong Kong's autonomy. It stipulates that as long as that autonomy remains genuine, the United States will recognize Hong Kong as a separate customs territory under the 1948 General Agreement on Tariffs and Trade (GATT) and its successor, the 1995 World Trade Organization. Hong Kong would also continue to enjoy such benefits as a separate textile quota. However, these benefits would be removed if, in the opinion of the United States, China did not honor its commitment to allow Hong Kong a high degree of autonomy.

The United States also took the unusual step of passing Hong Kong–specific immigration legislation in 1990. Provisions of the Immigration Act passed that year ensure that Hong Kong will not be amalgamated into China's immigration quota after 1997. More importantly, they allow recipients of immigrant visas to delay leaving Hong Kong until 2002, with the idea that that would encourage people to remain in Hong Kong beyond 1997 and, if things went wrong, they would still be able to get out.

Apart from these measures, however, it is unclear what else the United States could do to influence China's behavior after 1997. Given China's sensitivities regarding safeguarding its sovereignty and its opposition to what it considers to be interference in its internal affairs, there is always the danger that any American action could prove counterproductive, as was arguably the case with Britain's attempt to democratize the 1995 elections.

Hong Kong's symbiotic economic relations with China also mean that if the United States and other Western countries should ever impose sanctions on Beijing, Hong Kong will be hurt. The Hong Kong government has estimated that if Washington strips China of its most-favored-nation (MFN) trading status, the growth of the Hong Kong economy will be cut in half and some 90,000 jobs will be lost.

On a trip to the United States in spring 1996, Governor Patten warned the United States not to try to "help" Hong Kong by making continuation of China's MFN trading status conditional on the way Beijing treats Hong Kong.

In a major address in New York, the governor declared: "There are people who suggest from time to time that maybe the way the United States could best show its continuing concern for Hong Kong is to attach particular conditions on MFN, related, say, to our Bill of Rights or to the survival of our Legislative Council." However, he said, this was not helpful to Hong Kong but, in effect, would place Hong Kong in double jeopardy.

"I have to say to people who suggest that: thanks, but no thanks," he went on. "It's not a terribly good bargain for people in Hong Kong to tell them that on day one after the transfer they may lose their Bill of Rights or Legislative Council and, on day two, as a result, they may lose their job."

As to just what the United States can do to help Hong Kong,

Patten suggested that Americans remain concerned about the situation in Hong Kong after 1997. But, it would appear, there isn't much else that Americans can do to help.

Talking It Over

A Note for Students and Discussion Groups

This issue of the HEADLINE SERIES, like its predecessors, is published for every serious reader, specialized or not, who takes an interest in the subject. Many of our readers will be in classrooms, seminars or community discussion groups. Particularly with them in mind, we present below some discussion questions—suggested as a starting point only—and references for further reading.

Discussion Questions

Hong Kong is to be turned over by Britain to China in mid-1997, after over 150 years of British rule. Why is this taking place?

What are China's plans for Hong Kong after 1997? Do you think it will be dealt with differently than the rest of the country? Why or why not?

What are the prospects for the Hong Kong economy continuing to play a global role after 1997?

The author says that even without the 1997 issue, there would have been a "demand not only for accountability but for democracy" in Hong Kong. Explain why this is so.

In Hong Kong, on June 4, 1996, thousands gathered to remember those who died in the Tiananmen Square massacre in Beijing in 1989 and to demand that Hong Kong's freedoms remain untouched. Do you believe these demonstrations can do anything but antagonize the Chinese government?

In your opinion, will the Chinese try to make post-1997 Hong Kong a role model for Taiwan?

Reading List

Chan, Ming K., with Young, John D., eds., *Precarious Balance: Hong Kong Between China and Britain 1842–1992*. Armonk, N.Y., M.E. Sharp, 1994.

Chiu, Hungdah, Jao, Y.C. and Wu, Yan-Li, eds., *The Future of Hong Kong: Toward 1997 and Beyond*. Westport, Conn., Greenwood Press, 1987.

Cottrell, Robert, *The End of Hong Kong: The Secret Diplomacy of Imperial Retreat*. London, John Murray, 1993.

Davis, Michael C., *Constitutional Confrontation in Hong Kong: Issues and Implications of the Basic Law*. New York, St. Martin's Press, 1990.

Khanna, Jane, ed., *Southern China, Hong Kong, and Taiwan: Evolution of a Subregional Economy*. Washington, D.C., The Center for Strategic and International Studies, 1995.

Luk, Y.F., *Hong Kong's Economic and Financial Future*. Washington, D.C., The Center for Strategic and International Studies, 1995.

McGurn, William, *Perfidious Albion: The Abandonment of Hong Kong*. Lanham, Md., University Press of America, 1992.

————, ed., *Basic Law, Basic Questions: The Debate Continues.* Hong Kong, Review Publishing Company, 1988.

Morris, Jan, *Hong Kong.* New York, Vintage, 1989.

Rafferty, Kevin, *City on the Rocks: Hong Kong's Uncertain Future.* New York, Viking Penguin, 1991.

Roberti, Mark, *The Fall of Hong Kong.* New York, John Wiley & Sons, 1996.

Segal, Gerald, *The Fate of Hong Kong.* London, St. Martin's Press, 1993.

Welsh, Frank, *A History of Hong Kong.* London, Harper Collins, 1993.

Wesley-Smith, Peter, and Chen, Albert H., eds., *The Basic Law and Hong Kong's Future.* Salem, N.H., Butterworth Legal Publishers, 1988.

Wilson, Dick, *Hong Kong! Hong Kong!* London, Unwin Hyman, 1990.

Youngson, A.J., ed., *China and Hong Kong: The Economic Nexus.* New York, Oxford University Press, 1985.

A VALUABLE RESOURCE FOR KEEPING UP-TO-DATE

on key foreign policy topics in the news…
Subscribe to the **HEADLINE SERIES,** published four times a year.

Each issue ■ is about a major world area or topic
■ is written by an expert

ns,
st

HS 30 The Coming Plague
by *Laurie Garrett*, a health and science writer at *Newsday*.
... with *The Coming Plague* (Farrar, Straus & Giroux, 1994). Published April 1996. (72 pp. $5.95)

HS 30 U.S. Information Policy and Cultural Diplomacy
... professor emeritus at St. John's University, who has written extensively on the role of ... and ideology in U.S. foreign relations. Published February 1996. (64 pp. $5.95)

HS 30 Divided Korea: United Future?
... professor of international history and politics at Northwestern University. Published August 1995. (80 pp.)

HS 305 Japan's Democracy: How Much Change?
by *Ellis S. Krauss*, professor of political science at the University of Pittsburgh and a scholar of postwar Japanese politics. Published June 1995. (80 pp. $5.95)

Price per copy: $5.95 (double issue, $11.95)

Quantity Discounts: 10-99...25% off; 100-499...30% off; 500 and over...35% off.

Prepayment must accompany all orders plus $2.50 for postage and handling of first ...

Subscriptions One year...$20.00; two years...$35.00; three years...$50.00.

Write or call for a free catalogue

Foreign Policy Association
470 Park Avenue South
New York, N.Y. 10016-6819

(212) 481-8100 ■ (800) 477-5836 ■ Fax (212) 481-9275